Published by Creative Education
123 South Broad Street, Mankato, Minnesota 56001
Creative Education is an imprint of The Creative Company

Designed by Stephanie Blumenthal

Photographs by Archive Photos, Frank Balthis, James Blank, Richard Cummins, Grace Davies,
Image Finders (Jim Baron, Bruce Leighty, Mark Gibson), Gunter Marx, Paul McMahon, Richard Nowitz,
Kathy Petelinsek, Photri (Kit Breen), Tom Stack & Associates (Sharon Gerig)

Library of Congress Cataloging-in-Publication Data

Nieson, Marc.
Barns / by Marc Nieson.
p. cm. — (Designing the future)
Includes index.
ISBN 1-58341-189-5
1. Barns—History—Juvenile literature.
2. Barns—Design and construction—Juvenile
literature. [1. Barns.] I. Title. II. Series.
TH4930 .N54   2001
631.2'2—dc21   00-047454

First Edition

9 8 7 6 5 4 3 2 1

Cover, dilapidated barn;
p. 1, wooden barn in need of paint;
p. 2, barn in a wheat field;
p. 3, barn loft towering
above sunflowers

BARNS

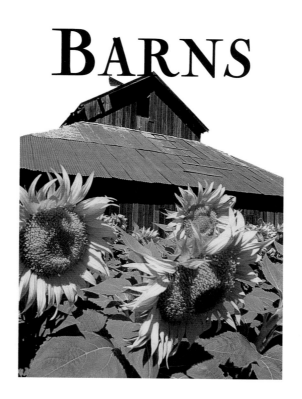

MARC NIESON

CREATIVE EDUCATION

Traditionally, barns are buildings used for storage on farms, but they are often much more. While many modern barns look like large metal garages or warehouses, barns built more than 60 years ago have a design all their own. Set back in the landscape along rural roads and often built of stone or wood, they look graceful and almost church-like. They're often worn and weathered, and some may even be leaning or in ruins. Yet these old barns stand as tribute to a time when farming dominated people's lives and livelihoods, and they continue to influence architects and designers.

Old barn in Irish countryside

Hieroglyphics showing ancient farmers at work

The old barns reflect the spirit of the people who built and worked within them—people who, at least from this distance in time, seem as strong, simple, adaptable, and enduring as their buildings. These people are part of a bridge between our prehistoric ancestors, who hunted and gathered their food, and the modern era. In a way, deep within the barn's shadows and stalls are housed not only grain and animals, but traditions of great know-how and innovation.

The use of special buildings to store grains dates back thousands of years, to the ancient civilizations of Egypt and Mesopotamia. The storehouses they built were known as granaries. Gradually, these buildings evolved to house animals as well.

The taming and raising of animals for food or work is an ancient tradition. At first, small groups of people with no permanent settlements moved their herds of goats and sheep great distances to let the animals graze. Over time, these herders began to settle, and in areas where the winters were harsh, their animals needed shelter. For centuries, these shelters were simple lean-to windbreaks built low to the ground and not necessarily meant to last beyond a season or two.

The oldest surviving grange barn in England is at Goggeshall, Essex, and was built around 1140.

An old barn in collapse

The Catholic Church influenced medieval barn design

It wasn't until medieval times that the barn began to take on its current shape and size. The word "barn" was adopted in the 10th century. It

> The huge Great Coxwell grange barn in Berkshire, England, was built in the mid-13th century and remained in use until 1966.

comes from the Old English words for "barley" and "closed place"—which describes the barn's early use. At the time, barley was England's principal crop. Also at that time, the Catholic Church had a vast amount of power and land. Both rich and poor paid the Church a tax on their earnings, which was usually 10 percent and paid in the form of grain. Churches built huge warehouses, called grange barns, in which to store the grain.

Not surprisingly, the Church also influenced the form these buildings took, which in many ways looked like cathedrals. The outer walls were often built of stone, and a strong, simple wooden structure inside helped support a steep roof. This created a large open space inside for the grain. Some grange barns from the 12th century still stand today.

Smaller granary barns also served large farms, and their forms were determined by local building materials and climate. In virtually every case, the barn's size, shape, and design have depended on its

Carved religious figures often adorned medieval barns

Weathered barn on Iowa farmland

functions. Barns combine form and function beautifully, and as farming practices have changed, the barn has changed to meet farmers' needs.

Barn building increased dramatically once large numbers of Europeans started to immigrate to the New World. The early North American colonists were a

mix of European nationalities—English, French, Dutch, German, Swiss, Swedish, Finnish, Danish, Polish, Italian, and Slovak. They spread into the countryside from the eastern seaboard. Almost all of them had to farm in order to eat, and they all practiced their own cultures' methods of barn building.

The traditional barn designs of these cultures varied a great deal depending on each nationality's

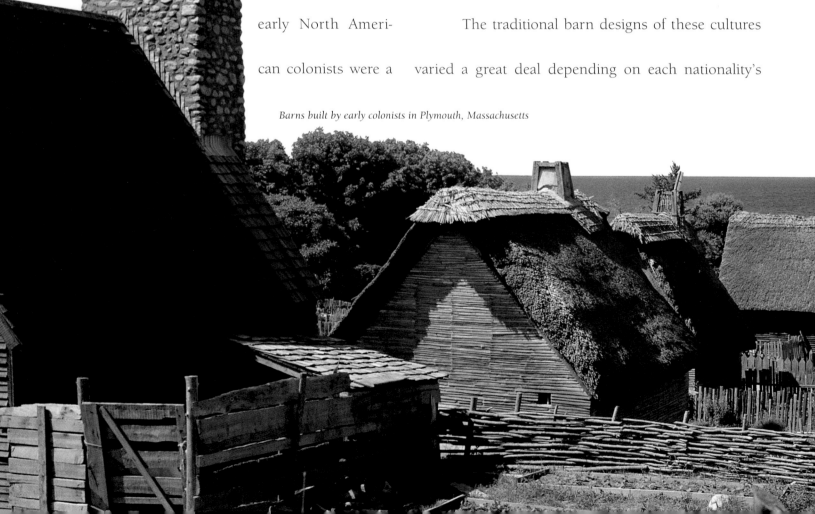

Barns built by early colonists in Plymouth, Massachusetts

A combination house and barn in the Swiss Alps

native land, weather, and farming traditions. Despite the differences among these settlers, their common needs tended to unite them. Neighbors helped one another build barns, sharing ideas and techniques in the process. As a result, new barn designs developed.

Above all, settlers wanted their barns to be soundly and solidly built. As they cleared the land of trees and rock, they used these handy, durable materials to build their barns and homes. North America's huge supply of tall hardwood trees allowed for larger, simpler barns than were possible in Europe, whose largest trees had long been harvested. Barns remained rectangular but were built with a variety of levels, doors, and passageways. Farmers were always looking for the simplest, most effective way to store

Since farm animals were so important to survival, early American barns were often built before the farmers' own houses. Farm families often lived in part of the barn until they could build houses.

Inside a large timber-framed barn

their crops and shelter their animals. Because work in the fields was so demanding and the weather so unpredictable, they had no time to waste.

The tools that farmers used to design barns were also plain and simple: a compass, a square, a straight-edge, and common sense. Before farmers could begin planning—let alone constructing—a barn, they had to choose the best location and placement. They had to think about the land's elevation and slope, otherwise the barn might flood. But they also needed to position the barn close to fresh water so the animals could drink.

Farmers also had to consider the weather to ensure the health and comfort of their animals, the protection of their stored grain, and the preservation of

Due to a lack of wood on the Great Plains, the first farmers moving west built lean-to sheds made of nothing but poles and straw for their cattle. The hay roofs provided both shelter and feed, and were replaced after each storm.

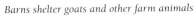

Barns shelter goats and other farm animals

A barn nestled in a Utah valley

the building itself. In the north, they had to anticipate where the wind was likely to pile snow in the winter to avoid finding the barn doors blocked by snowdrifts. Above all, the barn needed to be centrally located, because it was always the heart of farm activity.

The construction of early American barns was all done by hand. From felling trees with an axe to sculpting each timber for a proper fit in the barn's frame to the final driving of wooden pegs, barn building was hard and detailed labor. As a result, farmers strengthened not only their bodies, but their skills in carpentry and design. Once the foundations were laid and the lumber prepared, barns could be erected fairly quickly. Often the whole community gathered to lift the huge timbers into place. Barn raisings became social events, and when the work was finished, feasts and

dances often followed. Barns became not only function-

al buildings, but sources of personal pride for farmers.

One of the most interesting barn designs came

from the Shakers, a religious group that chose to live

separately from other settlers and loved designing

round objects—from hats to rugs to small boxes to huge

barns. The circular Shaker barns offered some signifi-

cant advantages in terms of strength and storage space.

For example, one round Shaker barn in Massachusetts

housed 52 head of cattle in 52 individual stalls around

Shaker-style stone barn in Massachusetts

The complex roof support structure of a round barn

its main floor. Another one in upstate New York was five stories high, and its circumference was the length of a regulation football field. Round barns, however, were very difficult to build.

Every barn's interior design had to make space for the farm's chores and needs. Traditionally, a large central area was reserved for threshing, or beating crops to separate the grain from the straw. Nearby areas were divided into compartments, generally called bays.

CONSTRUCTION

Metal nails weren't mass produced until around 1790. Before that, farmers either forged individual nails by hand or, more typically, used wooden pegs and pins to fasten their barns together.

The grain bin, or granary, occupied one bay and was tightly enclosed to keep out dampness and mice and rats. Straw and hay were stored in sections called mows.

Barns were often more than one story tall, and the entire loft served as a mow for storing hay and other feed. This became more common as farms began to keep more animals for meat, milk, and farm work. Bays on the lower level were then set aside as stalls for animals, who could be fed from above by tossing hay through a trapdoor. Nearby bays stored harnesses and supplies, or farm implements that involved the use of animals, such as wagons and plows.

Above the loft was the barn's roof, which protected not only the contents of the barn, but the building itself. The design of barn roofs varied according to need. The two most popular styles were the gabled

Barn loft used to store hay

Cupola atop a barn roof

roof, which was simple to build and shaped like a triangular tent, and the gambrel roof, which had an upper, relatively flat section and a lower, steeper part. Gambrel roofs offered greater storage and walking space within the loft.

Cupolas, small domes or towers with slatted openings for the passage of light and air, often sat on top of either style roof. Keeping fresh air moving in barn lofts was very important so the hay stored there wouldn't decompose and become prone to fire. Densely packed hay, if not sufficiently dry or cooled, could sometimes ignite. In the mid-1800s, farmers also began to

The colored glass balls often seen on barn lightning rods aren't just for decoration. When they're broken, they warn the farmer that lightning has struck.

Gabled-roof farm buildings in Wisconsin

attach lightning rods to their barn roofs as further protection against fire.

As a rule, early North American settlers were reluctant to decorate their barns. Many had religious leanings that favored humility. Most barns weren't even painted until farmers could excuse the act as a way of preserving the wood. Farmers made their own paint by mixing local red dirt with lime and cow's milk. The red color helped absorb the sun's rays in winter, which kept the farm animals warm.

Soon all farmers were painting their barns. Québecois (keh-bek-WAH) farmers in Canada covered their barn doors with brilliant colors and designs, and Pennsylvania Dutch farmers painted hex signs, which looked like quilting designs, on the sides of their barns. Eventually, advertisers turned barn sides and roofs into huge billboards for a wide range of products and services.

A barn decorated with hex signs

A barn billboard for an antiques shop

Drying tobacco leaves

Nothing changed barn design, appearance, and use more than the coming of the industrial age. The invention of such machines as mechanical threshers and tractors changed farmers' lives. They no longer had to rely on animals to do their heavy work. In time, hay was baled in round shapes that shed rainwater, so big interior lofts for storing hay were no longer necessary. Farmers could then reconsider how to use their barns.

As a result, barns stopped being buildings with many uses and became specialized buildings with a variety of new names. Some farmers had dairy barns that were only for housing and milking dairy cows. Others had sheep, swine, or poultry barns, or tobacco barns for storing and drying tobacco leaves. Many barns today are used to house farm machinery and vehicles instead of animals and grain.

Barn building materials have changed, too. Stone and brick foundations have been replaced by poured concrete. Premeasured steel framing and weatherproofed sheet metal have taken the place of hand-hewn timbers and roof shingles. Still, the barn remains a place for storage and shelter, and barns continue to be the center of farm activity.

Today, farming itself has become industrialized. Many farms are becoming large-scale businesses instead of small, family-run operations. Most small farmers can't compete with large-scale operations, and

Cows inside a dairy barn

Today, many traditional barns are being "reborn"

many have gone bankrupt trying. On the other hand, the family farmers who have managed to survive are finding that their children don't want to continue the farming tradition. At the same time, housing developments are steadily eating up farmland. As a result, each year thousands of the old timber and stone barns are sold and torn down.

Some of the old barns that survive, however, are finding new uses on small specialty farms. In some communities, old frame barns have been put to non-farming uses. Painters, sculptors, and actors were the first non-farmers to recognize the uses that a barn's open spaces could serve. They began converting the bays and lofts into workspace and living quarters.

Primitive timber barn interior

Members of an Amish community raising a barn

Now, more and more people are remodeling old barns into homes, studios, and even restaurants. Some are moving barns to other sites. Barns whose design or history is particularly important have been added to official historic preservation lists to make sure they'll be kept in their original forms and properly maintained for generations to come.

In recent years, the general public has become increasingly interested in barns of the past. Huge

D E S I G N

Basic American barn design changed very little from 1650 to 1850. Farmhouse design, however, changed dramatically during that time.

Historic barn restored to its original form

Solidly built stone-and-brick livestock barn

A lone barn on the Oregon landscape

crowds come to re-enactments of historic barn raisings, where knowledgeable carpenters wear period clothes and demonstrate old hand tools and the techniques of barn building. Tourists flock to historical restoration villages for a chance to see the farm buildings and practices of old. Even in the most modern cities, the earliest books that parents place into their toddlers' hands often teach the children about barnyard animals and chores.

Barns are fundamental to our history and con-sciousness. Their simple lines and shapes, their grace and integrity, embody a tradition that no other archi-tecture—at least in North America—can claim. Their stones speak of stubborn will and endurance. Their weathered timbers are reminders of the pristine forests that once covered the land and the skill and industry of the people who carved out lives from the frontier. It's no wonder these stately buildings continue to fas-cinate us and inspire our respect.

INDEX